Journeying through
Lent towards Easter

Journeying through Lent towards Easter

A course for personal or group use

Joan Brown SND

kevin
mayhew

First published in 2002 by KEVIN MAYHEW LTD
Buxhall, Stowmarket, Suffolk IP14 3BW
E-mail: info@kevinmayhewltd.com

© 2002 Sister Joan Brown, SND

The right of Sister Joan Brown, SND, to be identified as the author
of this work has been asserted by her in accordance
with the Copyright, Designs and Patents Act 1988.

Scripture quotations adapted from the Jerusalem Bible, © 1966,
1967 and 1968 by Darton, Longman & Todd Ltd and
Doubleday & Company, Inc.

Psalms adapted by Sister Jane Hughes, SND.

Quotations used in the Readings taken from *Sacraments*, Fr H. Lavery,
published and © 1982, by Darton, Longman & Todd,
1 Spencer Court, 140-142 Wandsworth High Street, London SW18 4JJ

9 8 7 6 5 4 3 2 1

ISBN 1 84003 988 4
Catalogue No. 1500549

Cover design by Angela Selfe
Photography by Sister Joan Brown, SND
Edited and typeset by Elisabeth Bates

Printed and bound in Great Britain

Contents

Introduction

'Once upon a time', as the best folk stories say, there was no Lent. Only in this case it is absolutely true. There was no season of Lent as we know it today. Slowly over the centuries, as the Church developed, there came the growing realisation that the Paschal Mystery, the passion, death and resurrection of Jesus Christ, was central to the life of the Church and Lent became a preparation for a worthy celebration of the Paschal Mystery when all Christians would be renewed by the life of the risen Christ.

Our Lenten journey is one of personal and communal renewal, a journey after which nothing should be as it was before, because after Lent we do not go back, we go forward renewed by the risen Christ, whose life, hidden within us, shines forth in our lives ever more fully.

We are reminded of St Paul's words of encouragement to the Ephesians which we can make our own during Lent as we pray for the life hidden within us to grow strong that Christ may be alive in us through faith until, with all the saints, we come to know the love which is beyond all knowledge and are filled with the utter fullness of God.

> *May God, out of his infinite glory, give you the power*
> *through his Spirit for your hidden self to grow strong,*
> *so that Christ may live in your hearts through faith,*
> *and then, planted in love and built on love,*
> *you will with all the saints have strength to grasp*
> *the breadth and the length, the height and the depth;*
> *until knowing the love of Christ, which is beyond all knowledge,*
> *you are filled with the utter fullness of God.*
> Ephesians 3:16-19

Strengthened by this joyful walk towards Easter we continue to grow in the strength of the risen Lord. Living and loving as Jesus showed us. Listening to his word and keeping his commandments.

Praying that the risen Christ, present with us, will lead us to the vision of unlimited truth and unfold the beauty of God's love for us.

We begin our journey into this vision of unlimited truth and the beauty of God's love when we respond to God's call to conversion and the invitation to journey joyfully with Christ through his passion, death and resurrection into the heart of God.

> *The God who loved us with so much love was generous with*
> *mercy: when we were dead through our sins he brought us to life*
> *with Christ . . .*
> Ephesians 2:4

The way we journey through Lent should cause those who see us to say: 'See, they know how much God loves them.' There is no room for misery and gloom during this joyful season for our God is full of tenderness, mercy and compassion; ever-present and with loving care guiding us, in our weakness reaching out to us, renewing our strength, healing us and leading us towards the dawn of a new day. This is beautifully expressed in the words of the prophet Isaiah:

> *Your light shall break forth like the dawn,*
> *your wound quickly healed,*
> *your justice shall go before you,*
> *and the glory of the Lord shall follow you.*
> *Call and the Lord will answer,*
> *cry for help and the Lord will say: 'I am here'.*
> *God will give strength to your bones.*
> *You will be like a watered garden,*
> *like a spring of water that never runs dry.*
> Isaiah 58:8-9a, 11b

With a tremendous burst of energy and activity new life bursts through after the death-like sleep of winter. The awakening of nature stirs us into action. Like the beloved in the canticle we too are called to 'come'.

> *My beloved lifts up his voice, he calls to me,*
> *'Come then, my love, my lovely one come.*

For see, the winter is past, the rains are over and gone.
The flowers appear on the earth.
The season of glad songs has come,
the cooing of the turtle dove is heard once more in our land.
The fig tree is forming its first figs and the blossoming vines give
out their fragrance.'
Song of Songs 2:10-13

As soon as Christmas is over, almost immediately we hear this call to 'come', we are given no time to settle down into a cosy rut.

Come, the winter is past.
Come, the rains are over.
Come, the flowers are appearing.
Come, the turtle dove is cooing.
Come, the fig tree is blossoming.
Come, the vines are giving out their fragrance.
Come, it is time to gather.
Come, it is time to prepare.
Come, it is time to set out on the joyful journey towards Easter.
Come, it is time to be signed on with the great sign of Christ, the cross.
Come, it is time to set out as a community on our journey towards new life.

Week 1
A heart made new

A heart made new

Reflection

There is a season for everything,
a time for every occupation under heaven,
a time to be born,
a time to die . . .

Lent is an invitation to be reborn, an invitation to die. An invitation to allow ourselves to be overwhelmed with God's love for us. An invitation to journey deep inside ourselves and come face to face with the wonder of our hidden being. An invitation to discover the mystery of who we are that Christ should gladly sacrifice himself for us.

O who am I, that for my sake,
my Lord should take frail flesh and die?
Samuel Crossman

Lent is an invitation to face up to our fears, a time to respond to God's call:

Come back to me, with all your heart, don't let fear keep us apart . . .
Gregory Norbert, OSB. From the prayer 'Hosea', © 1972 Benedictine Foundation of the State of Vermont, Weston Priory, VT.

An invitation to be:

Loved with all the heart of God.
To bloom like the lily,
to thrust out shoots like the poplar,
to have the beauty of the olive and the fragrance of Lebanon . . .
Hosea 14:6-7

Reading

The opening chord of the good news is that sin is not a terminal disease, not an incurable cancer. The whole of the

Gospels, the music and melody of Christ's teaching, is that sin is not the prevailing wind in the world. Forgiveness is the first reality. Many good people may never achieve this liberation; they let sin-consciousness become sin-obsession and they cannot know that joy so eloquent in St Paul, which he called the freedom of the sons and daughters of God.

Christ conveys what is hard to believe, that the sin in me is not decisive; that I can be reborn, restored to my origin and become one with God, become human by affiliation with the only human. 'You too can be one as I and the Father are one.' The man who said that used the pronoun 'I' and he is a man; he is our man, our symbol, our representative. He represents us to the Father and he represents the Father to us. He is the representative present among us. Nothing can separate us from his presence, not even the most shaming sin. This is the opening chord of the good news.
Hugh Lavery, *Sacraments*.

Discussion

- How did Christ value himself? Had he self-esteem?
- How did Christ value others?
- Can you think of anyone, alive or dead, who has or had self-esteem and freedom of spirit?
- In what ways would you say self-esteem and freedom of spirit are life-giving?
- Would it be true to say that they are the foundation of our rebirth?
- Why is self-esteem so important and why does honesty bring the blessing of self-esteem?
- From what enslavements does owning the truth set us free?
- Read the passage once more. What now strikes you in this passage?

Personal reflection

- Recall a time in your life when you felt appreciated. How has it helped your morale?
- How do you react when your self-esteem has been intentionally or unintentionally damaged?
- Are you able to forgive those who damage your self-esteem?
- Are you aware of damaging someone else's self-esteem?
- Recall a time when you experienced the joy of forgiveness.
- Is there anything you find hard to believe about forgiveness?
- What helps you to trust in the Lord's forgiveness?
- What do you value most about yourself?

'Nothing can separate us from his presence, not even the most shaming sin. This is the opening chord of the good news.'

A time for prayer

Light a candle and say together:

Lord, we have accepted your invitation to journey with you during Lent.

Scripture reading

Since you have been brought back to true life in Christ,
you must look for things that are in heaven,
where Christ is, sitting at God's right hand.
Let your thoughts be on heavenly things,
not on the things that are on the earth
because you have died,
and now the life you have is hidden with Christ in God.
But when Christ is revealed – and he is your life –
you too will be revealed in all your glory with him.
Colossians 3:1-4

Psalm 51

O God, you are so full of love and kindness.
As a mother patiently tends the wounds and bruises of her child
so I beg you to wash and heal the wounds of my sin.

I know when I sin
and I know when my sins offend you.
My conscience is uneasy when I remember the many times
I have turned against you, not following your commands.

God, you are the Creator of all things and my Creator.
Although I am unworthy of your love,
do not leave me to my own devices.
I need your Holy Spirit,
I need your love and your help.
Create in me, I beg you,
a heart that will rejoice for ever in your love.

Prayer

God who made me and knows me,
who created my innermost self,
who watched my bones take shape in my mother's womb,
who knows every fibre of my being,
who hates nothing you have created,
I thank you for the wonder of my being,
for the wonder of who I am.

Overlook my sins, let them fade like the morning dew.
Call me back to you.
Help me to know just how much you love me.
To rejoice in your great love for me whom you have created
even though I feel unworthy of your love.

Scripture to ponder

Ephesians 2:1-10; 5:1-20; Romans 8:14-17.

Week 2
A heart of prayer

LENT GROUP 2003.

journeying through lent towards easter.

WEEK TWO   A HEART OF PRAYER

Opening Prayers.

There is a season for everything
A time for every occupation under heaven
A time to be born, and a time to die.................

Lent is an invitation to live the life of the new heart. It is an invitation to journey more deeply, more intensely into personal and communal prayer. Prayer which costs no less than everything without fear, knowing that the God who calls us by name journeys with us.

Do not be afraid for I have redeemed you. I have called you by your name, you are mine. Should you pass through the sea, I will be with you, or through rivers, they will not swallow you up. Should you walk through fire, you will not be scorched and the flames will not burn you. For I am Yaweh, your God and your Saviour. Do not be afraid, I am with you.   (Is43; 2-3)

Each of us is called individually, personally, by name and by paths and ways pleasing to God. We respond to this call according to our heart's desire expressed in our prayer, like Jesus, who during his life on earth......

.......offered up prayer and entreaty aloud and in silent tears, to the one who had the power to save him out of death, and he submitted so humbly that his prayer was heard. Although he was Son, he learnt to obey through suffering, but having been made perfect, he became the source of eternal salvation for all who obey him.   (Hebrews 5;7-9)

We can take to heart the advice St. Paul gives to the Ephesians in his letter when he bids them to pray constantly.

Pray all the time asking for what you need praying in the Spirit on every possible occasion.   (Ephesians 6;18)

Hugh Lavery SACRAMENTS

God does not compel or coerce. God invites, persuades, attracts call but God does not impose. Each one of us is free to say 'no' or 'yes' to God. God is the one who lets us be. And God is the one who asks m to let the loved one be himself or herself. It is at this point we begin to understand the meaning of love and the meaning of sacrifice. True love is uncompelled. It is not forced. The dissolvent of love is possession. God does not possess me, God lets me be. If God possess me then we are pawns. If God owns us, we are servants. It Christ's first work to set us free, to call us not servants but friends, no retainers but a family of sons and daughters. God is the freedom tha creates other freedoms. The central and saving truth is that God doe not compel or force or frighten me. God loves me (I have called you I name, you are mine.....) To apprehend that God loves me is to see a things differently. The world is lit with glory.

And if God loves me, what should be the consequence ? One sentence in St. John is interesting because it seems to end the wron; way. It says ' If God so loves us....' Now one would expect the other half of the sentence to be ' so shouldn't we love God ?' But it is not. I ends ' then shouldn't we love each other '. St John sees the commar to love self, neighbour and god as one converging love. Love is indivisible. The one test of my love of God is earthed in the way I trea other people. 'If God so loves us should we not love each other ?

Discussion

A) Did Christ value prayer ?

B) Can you give examples of when Christ prayed and for what he prayed ?

C) Christ spoke in parables about prayer. Do you remember any of them ?

D) Is it possible to lead a Christian life and not pray

E) In what ways does prayer help us to see all things different ?

F) How you understand ' Prayer as the best mirror of heart and mind' ?

G) 'Pray constantly....' In what ways might it be possible to pray constantly ?

A heart of prayer

Reflection

There is a season for everything,
a time for every occupation under heaven,
a time to pray . . .

Lent is an invitation to live the life of the new heart. It is an invitation to journey more deeply, more intensely into personal and communal prayer. Prayer which costs no less than everything, without fear, knowing that the God who calls us by name journeys with us.

> *Do not be afraid for I have redeemed you; I have called you by your name, you are mine. Should you pass through the sea, I will be with you; or through rivers, they will not swallow you up. Should you walk through fire, you will not be scorched and the flames will not burn you. For I am Yahweh, your God and your Saviour. Do not be afraid for I am with you.*
> Isaiah 43:2-3

Each of us is called individually, personally, by name and led by paths and ways pleasing to God. We respond to this call according to our heart's desire expressed in our prayer, like Jesus, who during his life on earth:

> *. . . offered up prayer and entreaty, aloud and in silent tears, to the one who had the power to save him out of death, and he submitted so humbly that his prayer was heard. Although he was Son, he learnt to obey through suffering; but having been made perfect, he became the source of eternal salvation for all who obey him.*
> Hebrews 5:7-9

We can take to heart the advice St Paul gives to the Ephesians in his letter when he bids them to pray constantly; *'Pray all the time, asking for what you need, praying in the Spirit on every possible occasion'* (Ephesians 6:18).

Reading

God does not compel or coerce. God invites, persuades, attracts, calls, but God does not impose. Each one of us is free to say 'yes' or 'no' to God. God is the one who lets me be. And God is the one who asks me to let the loved one be himself or herself. It is at this point we begin to understand the meaning of love and the meaning of sacrifice. True love is uncompelled. It is not forced. The dissolvent of love is possession. God does not possess me, God lets me be. If God possesses then we are pawns. If God owns us, we are servants. It is Christ's first work to set us free, to call us not servants but friends, not retainers but a family of sons and daughters. God is the freedom that creates other freedoms. The central and saving truth is that God does not compel or force or frighten me. God loves me. (I have called you by your name, you are mine . . .) To apprehend that God loves me is to see all things differently. The world is lit with glory.

And if God loves me, what should be the consequence? One sentence in St John is interesting because it seems to end the wrong way. It says, 'If God so loves us . . .' Now one would expect the second half of the sentence to be, 'so shouldn't we love God?' But it is not. It ends, 'then shouldn't we love each other?' St John sees the command to love self, neighbour and God as one converging love. Love is indivisible. The one test of my love of God is earthed in the way I treat other people. 'If God so loves us should we not love each other?'
Hugh Lavery, *Sacraments.*

Discussion

- Did Christ value prayer?
- Can you give examples of when Christ prayed and for what he prayed?
- Christ spoke in parables about prayer. Do you remember any of these parables?

- Is it possible to lead a Christian life and not pray?
- In what way does prayer help us to see all things differently?
- How do you understand 'Prayer as the best mirror of the mind and heart . . '?
- 'Pray constantly . . ' In what ways might it be possible to pray constantly?
- Read the passage once more. What now strikes you from this passage?

Personal reflection

- When, where has prayer been most helpful to you in your life?
- When, where has prayer been difficult for you?
- What helps you to persevere in prayer?

A time for prayer

Light a candle and say together:

Lord, we have accepted your invitation to journey with you during Lent.

Scripture reading

Once Jesus was in a certain place praying and when he had finished one of his disciples said, 'Lord, teach us to pray, just as John taught his disciples.' Jesus said to them, 'Say this when you pray:
Father, may your name be held holy,
your kingdom come;
give us each day our daily bread,
and forgive us our sins,
for we ourselves forgive each one who is in debt to us.
And do not put us to the test.'
Luke 11:1-4

Psalm 63

O God, my whole being calls out to you,
'Stay with me'.
Without you my life is desolate and grim,
I am like somebody struggling through desert country
burned by the blazing sun and scorching wind,
seeking for water and cool shade and finding none.
Only you can give me the comfort and consolation I seek.

Your love means more to me that anything else in this life.
And so I worship you,
praising and thanking you for all your goodness to me.
In your love I find all that I long for:
the true peace and happiness that I seek.

At night, as I lie awake, my thoughts turn to you
who have never failed to love and care for me.
I rest peacefully, for like a mother, you hold me in your arms
and I cling closely to you trusting in your love.

Prayer

God of love, open our hearts to the sound of your voice.
You who say 'Whatever you ask in my name will be given to you.'
I am broken and in need of healing,
doubting and you call me to believe.
I am selfish and you call me to give and not to count the cost,
self-centered and you call me to reach out to others.
You call me to pray without ceasing,
to love others with the same love with which you love me.
God of love help me to believe in your love for me.
Help me to see all things differently, to see a world lit with your glory.

Scripture to ponder

Matthew 21:18-22; Mark 11:20-25; Luke 11:9-13.

Week 3
A heart of truth

A heart of truth

Reflection

There is a season for everything,
a time for every occupation under heaven,
a time for feasting,
a time to fast . . .

Lent is an invitation to respond to the sound of the trumpet calling the community to wholeheartedly turn back to God and to begin the solemn fast. It is an invitation to open our closed hearts to the tender loving mercy of God. It is an invitation to believe that God cannot help but be moved with pity for his people who express the truth of their heart, their longing for God, their hunger that will only be satisfied by the return of the bridegroom, by fasting.

And so all are called to the fast. No one is excluded.

> *Sound the trumpet in Zion! Order a fast, proclaim a solemn assembly, call the people together, the community, the elders, the children, even infants at the breast, bride and bridegroom . . .*
> *From this solemn gathering no one is excluded . . . all are invited to join in the prayer of the priests and ministers:*
> *'Lord! Spare your people.'*
> Joel 2:15-17

Why fast? It is the sign that we live in the joyful hope of the coming of the Lord in glory, the true sign of the faith professed in the heart. Jesus answers the questions of the disciples of the Pharisees on fasting.

> *Observing that John and his disciples were fasting some people came to Jesus and asked; 'Why is it that the disciples of John and the disciples of the Pharisees fast, but your disciples do not?' Jesus replied; 'The bridegroom's attendants would never think of fasting while the bridegroom was still with them . . . but the time will come when the bridegroom will be taken away from them and*

then they will fast . . .'
Matthew 9:14-15

We fast because we live in the time of invitation to the wedding feast, we live in the time of preparation. We live in the time when Jesus says to us, *'If you wish to be perfect, go and sell what you have, give the money to the poor and you will have treasure in heaven; then come follow me'* (Matthew 19:21).

Reading

People now ask if affluence brings beatitude, if possessions create happiness, if the good life consists in goods in over-supply . . . and the psalmist writes, 'The heavens declare the glory of God . . .' Poets write of a world charged with the grandeur of God and heaven in a wild flower . . . but for the world today this is becoming a lost vision . . .

The disease of the world is eye disease, an astigmatism which has narrowed vision that now we see only things as surface and are not satisfied. The great question is: 'What is the Good?' And the answer given is the thing which can be used. The last secular symbol is the status symbol . . . the symbol of affluence. The latest car declares not what I am but how much money I have. Once men and women are assessed by what they have, then they too have become just objects. So often the more you have the less you are.

The consequence of this surface understanding is superficial-ity and an interior emptiness. If the thing is the only reality then how can you live? Only by acquisition. Life is no longer being, but having. Love is no longer giving, but possessing.

A person is no longer to be loved, only used . . . It is hard to learn that what we earn is less valuable to us than what we are given . . .

Family, friends, life and love, these are given things, gracious things. Given to those open to their reception; seen only by those with eyes which can see 'heaven in a wild flower.' Christ loved the world. Christ saw the world as so loveable

he died for it. He asks me to see myself as called to serve and save the world. This asks for new vision and kind eyes . . . the vision and eyes of a person whose values are in tune with Christ's and relay Christ's generous attitudes . . .
Hugh Lavery, *Sacraments*.

Discussion

- Did Christ fast? Why?
- Is fasting referring only to fasting from food?
- Did Christ in his life on earth fast in any other way?
- Why is the importance of associating fasting with prayer and the sharing of goods stressed during Lent?
- Is it true to say that in responding generously to charitable appeals we give but we do not fast?
- How might fasting be the true sign of the faith professed in the heart?
- In today's society, how is fasting a sign that we live in joyful hope of the coming of the Lord in glory?
- Read the passage once more. What now strikes you from this passage?

Personal reflection

- Reflect on what has given, is giving, you the greatest happiness in your life.
- How is Lent inviting you to ask: 'What can I do to help bring about a more just sharing of this world's goods with the poor?'

A time for prayer

Light a candle and say together:

Lord, we have accepted your invitation to journey with you during Lent.

Scripture reading

My friends, think of the mercy of God and worship God in a way that is worthy of thinking human beings, by offering yourselves as a holy sacrifice, truly pleasing to God. Do not model your behaviour on that of the world around you, but let your behaviour change, modelled by your true heart. This is the only way to know the will of God and what is good and what it is that God wants, what is the perfect thing to do.
Romans 12:1-2

Psalm 131

O God, I do not look for earthly power or fame,
nor do I seek renown for learning or statesmanship.
I am no genius or artist endowed with creativity,
nor do I aspire to greatness.
Instead, God, I seek only to be loved by you,
to remain at peace like a baby in its mother's arms,
comfortable and sleepy after being fed.
Let me rest content in your presence, God,
trusting you to give me what I truly desire: your love.

Prayer

God of love,
in your tender mercy and compassion,
you have made us for yourself
and our hearts long to be with you.
Help us to rise to you in prayer on the wings of fasting
and almsgiving.
Give us a new vision and kind eyes
and the purity of heart to see heaven in a wild flower.

Scripture to ponder

Mark 12:41-44; Luke 21:2-4.

Week 4
A heart of love

A heart of love

Reflection

There is a season for everything,
a time for every occupation under heaven,
a time for giving love,
a time for receiving love . . .

To love is to be invited into the very heart of God. It is an invitation to become like God; to become equal with God who sees little but the good in us and forgives the little that is not good. Jesus tells us that he loves us as much as God loves him.

> *I pray for those who through their words will believe in me. May they all be one. Father, may they be one in us, as you are in me and I am in you, so that the world may believe it was you who sent me . . . and that I have loved them as much as you loved me.*
> John 17:20-23

Lent is the season of invitation to open our hearts to Our Lord's command, 'Love one another as I love you . . .' The season to love with the love of Christ whose human heart, filled with the love of God, loved us without exception even to completely emptying out his life for us.

> *As God's beloved children, try to imitate God, by loving as God loves, and to follow Christ by loving as he loves you, giving himself up in your place as a fragrant offering and sacrifice to God . . .*
> Ephesians 5:1-2

Reading

> The baptised are a body of people naturalised into Christ. They seek to live, not in isolation, but in true communion with God and people. They live as members of a body; not loners, but lovers. A way of life which is not easy.

Many pious people, it seems, prefer isolation. Isolation lowers demand. Religion becomes private: I and God in quiet conclave. Prayer is secrecy; conduct and observance of laws. Other people must not intrude and pride proclaims that the pious keep themselves to themselves. They accept, sincerely accept, one half of Christ's command, 'Thou shalt love the Lord thy God.' They do not accept its corollary, 'Thou shalt love thy neighbour as thyself.' Exclusion is strong in many people. Indeed the story of the Tower of Babel is revealing. And this temptation persists; to seek God by straight access, by hard and lonely endeavour. It is the spirituality of the loner. A spirituality keen on God but cool on people.

The Tower of Babel is an unfinished building. We cannot live except by communication with God and with other people. Individualism is natural, communion makes demands. Christ offers the hand of communion, human instinct declines to take it. To receive requires a new heart, a new spirit.

Hugh Lavery, *Sacraments.*

Discussion

- Christ in his relations with people showed that he loved and cared for them.

- What kind of people did he love?

- How did his love show itself?

- What effect did his love have on people?

- Are people still affected by his love?

- How do you understand the great commandment 'You must love the Lord your God with all your heart and your neighbour as yourself'? (Luke 10:27-28)

- How life-changing is the commandment? How world-changing?

- Would it be true to say that love of self is the fundamental preparation for being able to love anybody else?

- Is it necessary to experience being loved in order to love?
- Read the passage once more. What now strikes you from this passage?

Personal reflection

- To be loved by someone is to be made new again.
- Recall some moments of new life which you have experienced.
- How does love energise you to go out to others?

A time for prayer

Light a candle and say together:

Lord, we have accepted the invitation to journey with you during Lent.

Scripture reading

It can only be to God's glory, then, for you to treat each other in the same friendly way as Christ treated you. Jesus came to fulfil the promises made to the patriarchs. He also came so that non-Jews could know the one true God and thus he became a light to the revelation of the gentiles as Simeon had prophesied. As scripture says in one place: *'For this I shall praise you among the pagans and sing to your name.'* And in another place: *'Rejoice, pagans, with his people,'* and in a third place: *'Let all the pagans praise the Lord, let all the peoples sing his praises.'* Isaiah too has this to say: *'The root of Jesse will appear, rising up to rule the pagans, and in him the pagans will put their hope.'*

May the God of hope bring you such joy and peace in your faith that the power of the Holy Spirit will remove all bounds to hope.
Romans 15:7-13

Psalm 100

Let all the world praise and honour God,
and all nations strive to do his will.

As we joyfully place ourselves in God's presence,
we acknowledge with gratitude
that all we are and all we have
are his gifts of creation to each one of us.
He is like a shepherd and we are like the sheep he owns
following where he leads us
to find some nourishment and rest.

Let us give thanks as we praise God in churches, in temples
and in the quiet of our hearts
for gifts of infinite love and never-failing goodness.

Prayer

God of love and hope, hand in hand with Christ
we pray for a new heart and a new spirit.
A heart to love one another as you have loved us.
A heart to sing the praise of your glory for ever and ever.
A heart, filled with the power of the Holy Spirit
and boundless hope.
A heart filled with such joy and peace in our faith
that our love will know no bounds.

Scripture to ponder

Genesis 1:27; Colossians 1:15-20; 1 Thessalonians 4:12-18.

Week 5
A heart sincere

A heart sincere

Reflection

There is a season for everything,
a time for every occupation under heaven;
the season is now,
the time is ours ...

Lent is an invitation to turn wholeheartedly to God in the now of our lives. Lent is an invitation to hear Christ calling us to change and to be changed, to 'repent and believe the good news ...'

The idea of change is far from agreeable to most of us. We prefer to stay with what is familiar and comfortable, with what is safe, rather than to take risks. To settle down into well-worn ruts, resembling graves. But God's intention is that we should live, not bury ourselves alive:

> *I am now going to open your graves, my people, and lead you back*
> *to the soil of Israel. And you will know that I am God, when I*
> *open your graves and raise you from your graves, my people. And I*
> *shall put my spirit in you and you will live, and I shall resettle you*
> *on your own soil; and you will know that I, your God, have done*
> *this. It is the Lord who speaks.*
> Ezekiel 37:12-14

Inflexibility is a disguise for fear and fear of change is deeply rooted in us. We feel safe with sameness which lulls us into a false sense of security, and yet feel a restlessness; we are hungry, we are searching ... for what?

In Lent comes the call to 'taste and see that the Lord is good'. The call to look to the Lord and be radiant. The call to know and love God beyond our natural capacity. The call to enter into God's plan of loving goodness formed from all eternity in Christ. The call to glimpse the faithful and relentless love of God revealed at the wedding feast at Cana in the new wine. But there is no water into wine without change.

Reading

Everyone wants the life of wine and roses, and God will provide the wine as he provides the roses. But the new wine requires new wineskins. There lies the resistance; we want new wine, but we want the tried ways and the old wineskins. Christ sees this as impossible. We too must be changed, as water is changed into wine.

Throughout his life Christ intensifies the image and symbol of wine: 'I am the vine, and you are the branches.' What does this mean? . . . The life of the vine and the branches is one. One juice imparts life to both. Christ is speaking of an intimacy between God and humankind that exceeds expectation. . . . How? The final change is not water into wine. The final change is wine into blood. The lifeblood of Christ.

And the greatest change of all, Christ died to the life of human limitation. He was raised immortal, imperishable, to the life beyond restriction. Christ raised and renewed can impart his life totally . . .

Hugh Lavery, *Sacraments*.

Discussion

- What things did Christ want to change in his lifetime?
- What would be the consequences of the changes he proposed?
- What changes would we like to see take place in our lives, in our homes, our nation, our world?
- What action(s) might we need to take to bring about some of these changes?
- What risks would be involved?
- In what way is God calling us to change?
- Read the passage once more. What now strikes you from this passage?

Personal reflection

- How have you felt yourself called to change during Lent?
- How do you feel about these changes?
- How would you like to go on changing?
- What steps can you continue to take along the road that has brought you to the point of change?

A time for prayer

Light a candle and say together:

Lord, we have accepted the invitation to journey with you during Lent.

Scripture reading

All I want is to know Christ and the power of his resurrection and to share his sufferings by reproducing the pattern of his death. That is the way I can hope to take my place in the resurrection of the dead. Not that I have become perfect yet: I am still running, trying to capture the prize for which Christ Jesus captured me. I can assure you, my friends, I am far from thinking I have already won. All I can say is that I forget the past and strain ahead for what is still to come. I am racing for the finish, for the prize to which God calls us upwards to receive in Christ Jesus. We who are called 'perfect' must all think in this way. If there is some point on which you see things differently, God will make it clear to you; meanwhile, let us go forward on the road that has brought us to where we are.
Philippians 3:10-16

Psalm 126

When, God, you brought our exiled people home from captivity, it was almost too wonderful to believe.
We rejoiced and celebrated with merrymaking and feast.

Even those who did not share our faith in you
wondered at our great good fortune
and spoke about the marvels of our God
who rescued us from slavery.

God, there are still exiles and slaves in captivity,
free them from their oppressors.
Bring them flooding back to their homelands
as dried-up river beds overflow with life-giving water
from the winter rains.
Give them the joy that those feel
who, having laboured long, weary hours sowing seed,
rejoice when the grains of wheat they planted
produce crops rich for harvesting.

Prayer

God who makes all things new,
with sincere hearts we come to you with our fears
and our restlessness.
With joy and trust we turn to you,
knowing that whatever our sin may be,
even though the whole world condemn us,
you are always there, ready to set us free
from all that enslaves us
and holds us captive.
Through Christ, our Lord, you make of us a new creation.
With him, in the power of his resurrection,
may we walk joyfully to the end of our journey.

Scripture to ponder

Romans 8:18-39